ON THE WAY IN
English Edition

Pauline Lapointe-Chiragh

ON THE WAY IN
English Edition

ÉDITIONS HÉRITAGE DU CŒUR

Bibliothèque et Archives nationales du Québec and Library and Archives Canada cataloguing in publication

Lapointe-Chiragh, Pauline, 1942-

   [Au seuil d'une porte. English]

   On the way in / Pauline Lapointe-Chiragh ; translation, Guido De Volder, Lucie Battaglia.

      Translation of : Au seuil d'une porte."
      Issued in print and electronic formats.

      ISBN 978-2-9814374-9-5 (softcover)
      ISBN 978-2-9814374-8-8 (EPUB)

      1. Self-actualization (Psychology). 2. Dreams - Psychological aspects. 3. Lapointe-Chiragh, Pauline, 1942-. I. Title. II. Title : Au seuil d'une porte. English.

BF637.S4L3613 2018   158.1   C2018-942460-5
                                       C2018-942461-3

Cover design and Iilustration
Massoud Golriz

Drawings
Pauline Lapointe-Chiragh

English revision
**Guido De Volder, MA and Lucie Battaglia, B. trad.
Hira Masood and Evelyn L. Schofield, B.A.**

To contact the author:
Les Éditions Héritage du cœur
10, 8e Avenue, suite 802
Deux-Montagnes (Québec) J7R 0L7
www.heritageducoeur.com
heritageducoeur@outlook.com

Copyrighting: 4th trimestre 2018

             Bibliothèque et Archives nationales du Québec
             Bibliothèque et Archives Canada

Autres versions de cet ouvrage :

Au seuil d'une porte (nouvelle édition)
Lapointe-Chiragh, Pauline 2018
ISBN 978-2-9814374-4-0 (imprimé)
ISBN 978-2-9814374-5-7 (édition numérique EPUB)

On the way in Édition anglaise
Lapointe-Chiragh, Pauline 2018
ISBN 978-2-9814374-9-5 (imprimé)
ISBN 978-2-9814374-8-8 (édition numérique EPUB)

Au seuil d'une porte Tome 1
Lapointe-Chiragh, Pauline 2014
ISBN 978-2-9814374-0-2 (imprimé)

La version française du présent titre *Au seuil d'une porte* a fait l'objet d'une adaptation en format audionumérique DAISY pour les personnes ayant une déficience perceptuelle.
Bibliothèque et Archives nationales du Québec (BAnQ) : http://banq.qc.ca
www.vuesetvoix.com

The French version of this title *On the Way in* has been adapted in the DAISY audio-digital format for the visually impaired.
Bibliothèque et Archives nationales du Québec (BAnQ) : http://banq.qc.ca
www.vueselvoix.com

Autres ouvrages des Éditions Héritage du cœur :

Revivre de sa vie
Pyer, Jean 2015
ISBN 978-2-9814374-2-6

*To my grandchildren, Eve and Gabriel,
with the desire to prolong the existence of
their grandpa, departed without knowing them.*

TABLE OF CONTENTS

To tell the truth...

Here is the story of a life filled with awareness of the signs brought by events; some expected and others unusual.

This is also the story of our daily lives. The most ordinary occurrence can inspire reflection as well as research into what is essential, even down to the most intimate details. Everything becomes part of the story as soon as we decide to exercise care in what we do.

This is the story of a search for meaning amongst joys and trials, in dialogue with a wisely affirmed ideal of brotherhood.

This is the story of friendships and encounters, and even of travels, that keep love alive and lead to new connections.

This is the story of the night dreaming of the day and the day dreaming of the night, in a search for improvised freedom in accordance with events reflecting the same search for ideals.

This is the story of a boundary to be determined between the knowledge of the spirit and the challenge of the observer, who draws his attentiveness from his own approach.

It is, in the end, the felicitous meeting of narrative and tale, of reality and memory, of body and mind—the meeting of words and living memories.

Father Benoît Lacroix

Foreword

This book is the result of long reflection. Looking back on my days, I have seen the path of my life, an adventure through the silence of words.

I tried to clarify my memories, to recapture those who had faded. I revisited colourful landscapes rich in emotions.

I undertook this work in memory of Yousaf, my spouse for forty years, as well as in honour of my children, Sonia and Réjean, through whom I discovered the miracle of life, and of Réjean's wife France, who truly radiates love.

PART ONE

CHAPTER 1

A door opens

Born to provoke and charm,
Born to dare, have fun and astound,
Born to move mountains,
Born to speak, dream and shine,
And to spread the zest for life.

These words were written in the card I received for my 65th birthday. Is life meant to provoke, to spark reflection and bring about challenges? Or is it simply about letting feelings emerge and embracing their magic; about opening new doors and letting inspirations lead to renewal and hope? Do we need to confront life to grow and evolve, or develop ourselves according to our personality? I think that through experiences and the emotions they arouse, people discover themselves and find their true purpose in life.

These key questions continue to resonate in my mind. One night, I had the following dream:

Someone opens a door and leads me into a room with a peaceful atmosphere. I sit down and watch the tall, bright flame of a candle. Gradually, I focus on my breathing.
- I feel the air gently flow in and out.
- I feel calmness and peace grow within me.
- I feel my breath reach down into every fiber of my body.
- I feel my living body, one with the Universe.

As I wake up, I feel unusually at peace and a thought echoes in my mind. To grow old with grace, why not set free what vibrates deep within me? Sitting at the computer, I type these words: Why not write? I typed the statement once more, and then copy-pasted it on the screen. For no apparent reason, from this simple operation, the computer starts running ceaselessly. I try to close the file, but a message warns me that I might lose data. So, I wait. Then I finally understand the cause of the slowdown: the sentence was printed over and over, filling 720 pages!

What a coincidence! Even the sentences on the computer screen appear to be in harmony with me. I see them as a sign of destiny, a harbinger of a fresh start. Some ideas ignite and give me impulses. I become a fireball of enthusiasm. This project to write a collection of my experiences enlivens my life.

As I size up the words, I initiate myself to their power. They warm my heart. New thoughts germinate in me and my mind comes to life. This activates my thirst to communicate. It gives me strength and the desire to push myself forward.

This challenge gives me the opportunity to nurture the little girl who lives inside of me, this misunderstood child who appears strong on the outside, but is so fragile on the inside. So many memories live within me. While recounting them, I feel hope and deliverance. In this way, by the power of words, I want to demystify some periods of my life.

Writing opens a door to new inner territories, leading me into a quest for truth using the magic of words, letting them vibrate and resonate to better hear their echo. After all, self-conquest is the first and noblest of all victories. As Confucius said: "He who does not understand the value of words, will never understand humankind."

❧ ❧ ❧

I strongly believe that everyone, at one time or another, encounters circumstances that require major, even dramatic personal change. So, when my husband died, I not only lost a spouse, but also a friend, a confidant, someone with whom I shared my existence for forty years.

Yousaf, this man who came from far away, opened wide the doors of his heart to me. By uniting the beauty of our respective worlds, by tasting the flavours of the East and of the West, we learned so much from each other. Our different universes were, at the same time, complementary.

Finding myself alone at the age of 63, I had to learn to live differently, to take in the transition and to live it step by step.

In addition to coping with the death of a loved one, I moved closer to my own destiny with the physical and psychological separations that would follow. I had to let go of a profession practiced for many years, leaving my naturopathic school and all my precious students and friends. Writing proved to be a way to close the loop, to capture the essence of my solitude, to give it new life, much like the caterpillar becomes a butterfly.

I also cherished the desire to leave a memory with my grandchildren, who never had the chance to know their grandfather, a man so special in my eyes. I wanted to pass on to them what emanated from him, his courage and his dignity, while allowing them to uphold their heritage.

Yet first, I had to take another step. I had to become familiar with the city, choose what would become my home, discover the area and location best suited to my needs. All the while, I would be taking the path of freedom, surrendering to the natural flow of life, removing all possible constraints and making my home a haven of peace.

I had to learn to forget the life of the suburbs. I had to say goodbye to my car and get accustomed to using public transportation while carrying my backpack; in short, I had to become a pedestrian. Even if being alive means adapting continually, all adjustments disrupt our existence for a moment.

With the consent of my adult children, I also went through this period of grief and transition thanks to travelling. During a trip to visit my step-family members, I decided to go solo and explore parts of Europe and the East. I needed to find myself among my husband's people, to surround myself with those who had also loved him. Being close to them, I found a part of him again; feeling his presence comforted me.

My need to belong was as necessary as the cultural contact and moral support. Alone in Canada, I was a woman without a spouse, and Sonia and Réjean were fatherless children. Upon my return, I was able to tell them that we had a lovely family scattered all over the world and eager to welcome us. This pilgrimage helped me move forward.

❧ ❧ ❧

As these changes happened very quickly. I felt exhausted and in great need of regeneration. That's when a memory came to mind: my mother had once stayed at a spa in Romania and, upon her return, she was radiant, completely transformed.

While continuing to question myself, I began seeking renewal. The goal was no longer to explore the Spice Route, but rather to learn about ancient therapeutic methods. My destination was Romania. I wanted to take the opportunity to enjoy the benefits of the sea, its coastal resources, as Cleopatra did in her time. And here I am traveling again! Spectacular landscapes, mountains and majestic waterfalls will be forever etched in my memory, as well as the monasteries made famous for their fifteenth-century frescoes. By spending some time there, I was able to clear my mind. It was a total immersion—cultural, historical and mystical at once.

Amid my solitude, I had time to filter some of the events of my past. This helped me perceive what thrilled or fascinated me. I thought, why not go a step further and live my secret passion of travelling? Why not organize trips aimed at preventing illness and promoting health, relaxation, culture and entertainment?

Further to this reflection, I invite you to let these words sink in and draw encouragement from them:

• Provoke, not to cause a reaction, but to surprise by exposing a relevant point of view.
• Charm those you love by bringing forth the light hidden within you.
• Dare to be brave; excel by taking that one decisive step to realize your dreams.
• Enjoy the game of life, embellish it, forget about time—entertain and reinvent yourself.
• Be astounded and find wonder in your talents and successes.

• Move mountains. Stay tuned to your inner voice, who encourages personal inspiration and spontaneous surprise.

• Express ideas, develop your thoughts and get inspired by way of your imagination and creativity.

• Dream about the unexpected, let your thoughts wander, discover new realms, go where the sun illuminates new skies.

• Shine, let forth the inner flame like a bright beacon; it lives in each of us.

• Spread the joy of living, irradiate through your gaze everything that emanates from your heart.

• Open your thoughts and beliefs to accommodate feelings of peace, abundance and love. Become the master of your life.

The impossible becomes possible for whoever explores life inspired by the laws of the universe, without rushing and while enjoying the freedom to learn, to grow, to give, to receive, to laugh and to love.

CHAPTER 2

Rediscovering my youth

On my father's side

My paternal grandfather, Léandre Audet (called Lapointe) and his wife, Eugénie Simard, moved from Baie-Saint-Paul at the end of the nineteenth century and settled in Saint-Cyriac, a village north of Lake Kénogami. In 1924, the parish was flooded due to the construction of dams by the Chicoutimi pulp mill. Thus, at the age of 22, my father Jos-Nil left his hometown and moved in with his parents, in Saint-Cœur-de-Marie.

The 1920s were promising. My grandfather invested in some land, hoping to see his children settle near him. While he and my uncles worked on logging sites, my father took care of the farm. He quickly took a liking to his work. He was interested in farm work, yet preferred other related tasks: organization, interaction with people, purchases and sales.

The farm, the forest, the business... From 1928 to 1931, it was Jos Nil's turn to work onsite as a lumberjack. He would work as a timber carrier, helped by his horse. From that period of his life, he holds memories of hard and demanding labour, where technique was often far more important than simple brute force. Thanks to the contribution of every member, in the early 1930s, the Lapointe family paid off the mortgage on their land.

The 1930s were difficult years; the global economy was suffocating. Yet my father still managed to develop his farm. Slowly he brought about changes, transformed some buildings, and eventually became the owner of a slaughterhouse. With my mother Germaine, he concocted recipes for blood sausages which soon became in high demand. The wholesale meat business began in Saint-Cœur-de-Marie, Alma and

Saint-Bruno, and later spread to Jonquière and Chicoutimi. This expansion did not satisfy him, as he was further attracted by the county of Lac-Saint-Jean Ouest.

In 1951, my father saw another important step in the diversification of his business. Jos-Nil bought a grocery store, slaughterhouse, butcher shop and delicatessen in Normandin. With the addition of retail to a wholesale meat business, the commercial enterprise Jos-Nil Lapointe et fils grew up to twenty employees. The Steinberg grocery chain in 1954 gave him an award of excellence for his blood sausage. For the next twelve years, the Normandin slaughterhouse was the sole supplier of Steinberg stores in the Saguenay. The retail market also developed to meet the needs of the growing community. His business, traditional at first, gradually expanded to become a modern company.

My father was quite friendly with his employees. Everyone attended his Wednesday morning luncheon. He talked about everything under the sun, always with great enthusiasm. He also served two terms on the city council of Normandin.

My father was an avid nature lover. His favourite animal was the horse; he always had at least one. From 1936 to 1954, he developed an interest in horse racing. At that time, he owned three young stallions that ran on the Jonquière racetrack. He often rode as a jockey himself. A few weeks before his death, he parted with his last pony.

He also had a natural gift for meteorology; he could look up at the sky and follow the signs to read what Mother Nature was preparing for the days to come. He also had such excellent manual dexterity—all he needed was a pair of scissors and a piece of cardboard, and he could create a paper horse. He always had many new projects in mind.

A lover of freedom, he believed in the virtues of free-market economy. His unrelenting commitment led him to clarify the Quebec law governing the sale of beer. At the time, the authorities hesitated whether to allow the sale of beer in grocery stores or to put it in the hands of municipal control. After three times in court, my father won. Today, all grocers and citizens in Quebec still benefit from the changed regulation.

My father was a fourth-degree member of the Knights of Columbus for about twenty years. He took great pleasure in travelling by sleigh to participate in the *guignolée* (food drive) during Christmastime. While picking up Christmas baskets, food, toys and treats, he took a shot of caribou (an alcoholic drink), as was the custom then. His ride home was always joyful.

He left me the memory of a man who cherished life.

On my mother's side

My grandfather belonged to the twelfth generation since his family arrived in Canada. Trefflé Gilbert had three children from his first marriage in 1894. After the death of his wife, he remarried and had thirteen more children. Finding himself widowed once again, he took a third wife.

In 2001, when Saint-Cœur-de-Marie merged with Alma (Lac-Saint-Jean), the toponymy committee selected the names of some ancestors from the founding families to name public places and roads. The Trefflé-Gilbert avenue was named in memory of my grandfather, a landowner who had contributed significantly to the development of the parish.

I have fond memories of the first three years of my childhood, which I spent alone with my mother while my sisters attended school. I enjoyed watching my mother knead bread on the bread bin. She cooked with love for her brood, baking pies and cakes by the dozens. Everything was delicious and fragrant.

Like all women in those days, she made butter and prepared her own yogurt to use in desserts or salads. She also used sour milk to prepare what is today called kefir; the whole family enjoyed its virtues. At the beginning of the summer season, she made rhubarb jam. Then at the end of the season, she prepared wild strawberry jam.

My mother also made soap and skillfully mended our clothes.

As for medicine, my mother reminded me of a real chemist: she gave us syrups for colds and coughs, remedies for toothache and to remove worms, liniments, mustard plasters and relief for asthma attacks. All this was no secret to her. Furthermore, she knew how to prepare infusions from the medicinal herbs in her garden.

My father followed the example of his horses' survival instinct to provide additional knowledge to my mother. He explained how they rolled in mud to heal a wound. My mother took his advice in preparing plasters and poultices for us to use. Today, the health benefits of clay are widely recognized: rich in minerals, it can activate the body's natural healing processes.

I undoubtedly owe my interest in preventive approaches, both for physical and mental health, to my parents. I do not remember ever seeing the doctor come to the family home during my youth.

It was later that I came to admire my mother's crafting skills. I still have her tortoise-shaped fabric Tic Tac Toe game. One Christmas, she offered each of us a decorative piece made of ceramic: a mobile from which hung birds flapping their wings, a promise of new life.

◆ ◆ ◆

I wish I had the soul of a poet to shine a better light on my memories, but still I try my best to present childhood memories that have coloured and shaped my life.

All the elements of nature were represented in me and my siblings: fire, earth, air and water. The atmosphere at home soaked up all the colours of the rainbow. Such a range of emotions would make my parents proud, or on other occasions, cause them dismay. Our moods did not remain silent; they influenced the climate of the family like a form of psychic weather.

I did not always know where to turn. Sometimes, we all got on one another's nerves. But the storm always died down. The sun reappeared; smiles and enthusiasm became contagious. Each of us enlivened the atmosphere in our own way.

One day, I decided to dive into the history of Quebec. During these explorations, I was well surprised to find a key to decipher my past. I realized the impact and the role of finances in my family life. This influence was obviously felt by the children according to their birth order and the context in which they had grown up.

My parents got married on August 23, 1933, and had nine children between 1934 and 1951. My father was ten years older than my mother. I was born in the country on August 19, 1942. Since my mother was working in the raspberry field when I began pushing out, my birth was a kind of unexpected harvest. I came into the world before the arrival of the doctor. Fortunately, one aunt took on the role of impromptu midwife.

At that time, our primary school teacher taught all levels, one after the other, from the first to the seventh grade. All schoolchildren under fourteen in our family would attend the same class.

When I turned 10, we moved to Normandin, about 95 kilometres from my birthplace. Our father then purchased a grocery and butcher shop with a delicatessen and slaughterhouse. His work became his main motivator in life. To meet the needs of his customers, he traveled two days a week through the Saguenay-Lac-Saint-Jean area. He could naturally find a balance between social life and work; his clients became his friends. He rarely complained about being too busy.

But for me, the adjustment was difficult. Leaving a country school and having to integrate into a regular classroom was a shock. I could no longer stay isolated, because this new form of learning required constant participation. After dictation, I would be corrected by my right-hand neighbour, who then orally reported the number of mistakes. This approach was a real nightmare for me. Being dyslexic, I confused the letters "b", "p", "d" and "t". I also had to struggle to study grammar rules and the list of prepositions and conjunctions. As for catechism, we were told to line up to form two teams in separate rows. The teacher asked a question; if the student didn't know the answer, he was sent back to the end of his row. Then it was the turn of the opposing team to give the right answer. During this competition, each was trying to help his team to win.

I also had to get used to our new family home. A single door separated us from the grocery store. The bedrooms were located on the upper floor.

◆ ◆ ◆

When we arrived in Normandin in 1951, my two older sisters had just finished their studies at the Jonquière boarding school. They worked at the grocery store until they left the family home. In the summer of 1957, the family solemnly celebrated a double wedding. In my teenage heart, everything seemed so easy for my sisters. My father, now a public figure in the village, was living his years of prosperity. At that time, my other two sisters were studying at Notre-Dame-des-Laurentides, in the teacher training establishment and family institute. For my father, it was only natural that another one of his daughters should take over the business. Since I had not yet committed to studies, I was selected. But I felt out of place, so the following January, I decided to enroll for night school, along with a friend who was in a similar situation.

◆ ◆ ◆

The Alcan strike

A few months later, the first and biggest strike in Saguenay began. At that time, 7,000 members of the aluminium workers union were employed by Alcan in Arvida. The region was recognized as one of the most prosperous in Quebec: wages were high, and the cost of living was relatively low. This strike lasted four months. Large families were not prepared to cope with such a hardship. The strike had an economic impact on all businesses on the outskirts of the Alcan plant and left wounds in the community.

Very soon, households began to experience financial difficulties. Regarding mortgage, arrangements were made with banking institutions. But things were different with day-to-day expenses such as grocery bills. It was a painful time for my father, since a part of his clientele lived in the Saguenay region. Often, the bailiff's visit would startle him, as it usually brought bad news: one or more bankruptcies among his customers.

This economic situation affected my father's life in many ways. He had difficulty managing this chaos. The stress generated by the financial crisis permeated the atmosphere with tension. During those difficult years, I shared both my family and work life with my parents. I lacked privacy. Unlike my older sisters, I never had the chance to know my father in his successful years. The difficulties were more than I could handle. The grocery store was not only the heart of the neighbourhood, but also a big part of my heart.

It was therefore with great determination and courage that my father continued to believe in himself. He took up the challenge to come out winning as time went on.

❧ ❧ ❧

The child, his birth order and role among siblings

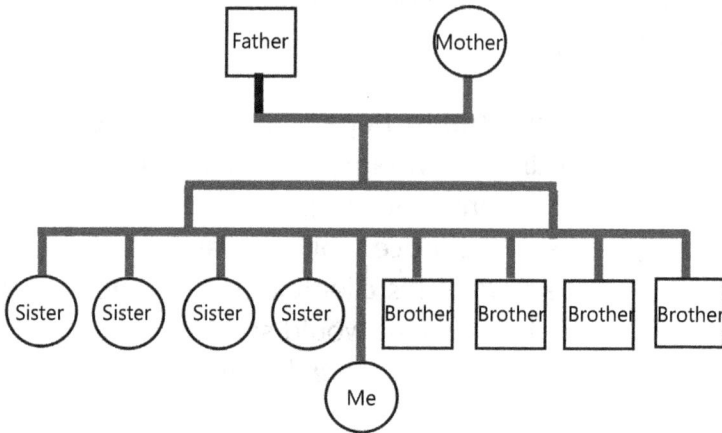

I am the fifth child in my family (see the family tree). I feel that my place in the order of birth has had a decisive influence on my life. Born between four sisters and four brothers, I did not always know if I was a girl or a boy, since I never seemed to belong to either group. But in fact, each group had a strong influence on me.

Within a household, each has a vision of what he or she represents. It is within the family unit that we take our first steps; this mini-society has prepared me to face the outside world.

For my part, I have maintained a keen interest in what exists beyond the visible world and in human ideals. The French neurologist, psychiatrist and psychoanalyst Dr. Boris Cyrulnik, known for developing the concept of "resilience", says: "A child never has the parents of his dreams. Only children without parents have dream parents."[1]

◆ ◆ ◆

The Dolbeau Carnival was the event that best represented the colours of Lac-Saint-Jean; it was an ideal place to meet and greet. Reminiscent of the winters of yesteryear, it entertained the population in a healthy and enjoyable way. Thanks to the efforts of many collaborators, each year the Carnival was a resounding success. It was organized in seven villages across the region; each named a Duchess, one of whom would become Queen. Residents made it a point of honour to build a snowman, an ice monument or a snow sculpture to decorate the front of their house.

The official opening began as *Bonhomme Carnaval* (the snowman mascot) arrived by helicopter with the Carnival Queen. Activities abounded: visits to different cities and hospitals in the area, days of activities with children, downhill torchlight skiing, processions on ice and dances around the fire. Carnival Boulevard housed even more events: Western breakfast, Canadian supper, hockey and broomball games, snowshoe racing, sleigh rides and skating. The smile of Bonhomme, the king of the celebration, was contagious.

At 19, I was lucky to be nominated as Duchess by the committee in Normandin. In 1961, I was elected Carnival Queen. From the top of my ephemeral throne, I gained a whole new perspective of the outside world. This fresh air gave me a new aspiration: going up in altitude to change attitude. Hope gave me an impulse to go beyond my limits.

In the 1960s, I excelled in the art of dance. Let me tell you a secret: my first criterion for choosing a suitor was that he had to be a good dancer. Yes! Dance is an art of movement that allows the expression of thought while opening us up to feelings, intuitions, senses and instincts. Through spontaneity and the expression of feelings, dance connects us with all five senses. By fluctuating movement between balance and imbalance, from the breath of life, dance grounds us. It helps us take our place and center ourselves again.

Elvis Presley's music was therapy to me. I let myself be swayed by the musical rhythm of his songs. Dancing rock and roll was a real escape and an explosion of energy! I particularly remember my red dress with spaghetti straps; I felt resplendent with my crinoline enhancing my movements. I also let myself be carried away by the music of the words when my body pulsated to a slow tune such as Love Me Tender. And what emotion I felt when I flew into a waltz. It made me feel like I defied gravity! As Plato said, "Dancing is divine in its nature and is the gift of God."

Together with a friend, I formed a folk-dance group, which gave me two opportunities to take intensive dance workshops in Montreal. This pleasant and practical activity allowed me to develop many friendships through correspondence. I enjoyed discovering these unknown worlds. New friends and exchanges of ideas warmed my heart.

◆ ◆ ◆

By scrolling through these memories, I took pleasure in stretching out time to unravel the fabric of my childhood and reconnect with my aspirations.

Love me tender,
Love me true,
All my dreams fulfilled.
For my darling I love you,
And I always will.

CHAPTER 3

Departure

At the age of 24, having only known fleeting romances which I took as signs of fate, I decided to leave the family nest and fly to another world.

I harbored the secret desire to discover the person inside of me, who seemed inexistent. This person bore the name "Pauline" but was constantly called *"pas Line"* (not Line). Throughout my childhood, the sound of my name grated on my ears. From my earliest years, when I would listen to the radio with my mother, some names would charm me. I thought that when I became an adult, I could choose a new one. My mother let me dream.

My first name was a nuisance to me, somewhat of an embarrassment. Its mispronunciation would put a damper on my ambitions. Its echo resounded as a daunting joke.

I had to leave Lac-Saint-Jean, the North and the cold to head south. I chose to discover new things and fully welcome the gifts of life. With my heart full of hope, I signed up for an intercultural exchange with an English-speaking girl from Woodstock, Ontario. She visited us first. Then it was my turn to spend time with her family. What a change! She only had a younger brother, and her father was a pharmacist. This happened during the school holidays. I felt very blessed to discover a new universe.

Time went by too quickly; I could not stop it. When I said goodbye to my new friend, a great sadness came over me, but I left with the hope of seeing her again. I travelled by train, with a four-hour stopover in Toronto's Union Station, while I waited for the connection to Montreal and Lac-Saint-Jean. I was dreaming up a strategy to ensure my return to Ontario.

Back in the day, a large trunk with a fabric lining served as a bride's trousseau or as luggage for travellers. I decided to leave my trunk at the station for a month to keep ties with the place.

Since the eldest of my brothers was now ready to take over at the grocery store, I continued searching for ways to leave the nest. An employment agency informed me that a Toronto family was looking for a nanny. This comforted my parents, because the position offered a safe place to live as well as a salary. Although it was perhaps not the best choice, I took advantage of this first opportunity.

Everything was different from my hometown. I was once again in Ontario. However, it was not like my vacation in Woodstock where I was so well surrounded.

In my hometown, even without knowing the street names, I could easily show a visitor where to go: "Walk straight ahead to the third street, turn left. Two blocks down, turn right and you'll see the third house with a red door." Here in the big city, it was not enough to notice a bank as a landmark, since another one stood right down the street. Despite being constantly pushed around in crowds and on public transit, I felt such a great loneliness. How could I develop a sixth sense to perceive warning signs and break free from my fears?

I felt like I was sinking into icy water. I had to break the ice, or even melt it. In high school, I had learned the basics of the English language, but upon my arrival in an English-speaking province, everything was different. I could hear the words, but I did not understand. No wonder, since the nun who taught us English at Notre-Dame-du-Bon-Conseil had quite limited knowledge—she taught us that "a" in English is pronounced "é" as in French. So, we repeated "I héve, you héve", and so on. With this pronunciation, I obviously had better luck making myself understood through written notes or gestures than with words. On the other hand, this major barrier did persuade me to enroll in an English course.

In the meantime, I had made friends with a girl named Nina and quit my job as a nanny. Together, we rented an apartment. What a blessing to enjoy my first home on my own, as modest as it was!

My openness to the world

I went back to school, where I discovered a new life rich in colour and contrasts. I felt alive again, and delighted to meet people from all continents, with different cultures and mindsets. It was as if I was borrowing a piece of their universe to enrich mine. To enhance each of my encounters, I worked hard at mastering the English language. Many times, in my sleep, I dreamed that I was speaking English fluently. And I remember trying to prolong these moments upon waking.

I learned more than just the English language; I awoke to life. Public speaking was part of my course curriculum and forced me to face my demons. All students had to introduce themselves, expressing childhood memories in their own words and speaking about their city and country of origin. These stories were inspiring because we discovered interesting similarities between one another.

We all came from different places. At our young age, we were ready to offer our hearts to experience better days. A common ideology united us. It was easy to trust each other and communicate openly. This human warmth was contagious; it gave the impression that together, we formed a family. Each sought to discover the other, and when words failed us, we conversed through our eyes.

Curious by nature, I was simply bewildered by this gift of destiny. I had embarked on a fascinating adventure. I discussed with my peers; I observed and analysed them, so I could better understand human beings. This approach allowed me to further explore the world of the senses. I wanted to turn my sensitive side into an asset: a special ability to develop, which would enhance my intuition and allow me to passionately live in the present moment. I did not simply live. I existed, down to every fiber in my body. I learned to observe events step by step. My conscience was awakening to personal and general freedom, as well as to compassion.

To improve my quality of life, I found a part-time job as a cashier, a job which my father had taught me to do so well. But then, another surprise awaited me.

CHAPTER 4

A decisive encounter

At work, a tall and slender, dark-skinned and handsome man with a beaming smile was sitting alone at a table, focused on his newspaper. Right from the first glance, he turned my heart upside down. It was precisely at that moment that I understood why I had never known true love: he was the one I was waiting for. But how could I win his heart? I felt so limited by language... One day, however, we established contact through our eyes. And that is where it all began.

He spoke to me: "It's unfortunate that you work weekends." I immediately replied confidently: "Next Sunday, I'll be free." He then asked me if I would prefer to go to the movies or out to dinner. I answered promptly: "To the movies." With my limited vocabulary, it was easy to understand my choice.

We planned our date for early in the afternoon. After the movie, he offered to get drinks at a terrace restaurant located on the 33rd floor of a nearby building. We communicated more with our eyes than with our words. A violinist came to our table to play a melody. Such an atmosphere awakened my senses! The romantic music reminded me of my childhood, when we enjoyed listening to one of my father's employees playing the violin. I had just shared a special moment that I hoped to relive. To avoid boring Yousaf, I told him I was already busy for the evening. In fact, I wanted to be alone, for I did not want to dim the flame that I had seen in his eyes.

Early in our relationship, he became my tutor; during our meetings, he corrected my schoolwork. Later, he became my protector. Knowing that I was still going through a period of survival, he offered me fruit each time he came to visit. To put me at ease, he explained: "It costs next to nothing more to buy a basket instead of a pound." Sometimes he would offer his tips on fine cuisine. I then discovered the delights of a sophisticated palate. He made me acquainted with the world's spices and flavors, and I savoured every meal with pleasure. His attention constantly surprised me.

His eyes reflected the softness of his heart. Yousaf knew how to read my moods. He also knew how to deal with my bold, spontaneous, and often naive nature, and my tendency to enjoy surprise and feel emotion like a child.

Being born in a warm country where he never had to brave cold winters, he had a hard time understanding how women could continue to wear pantyhose, even in icy weather. One day, he surprised me with cotton tights to keep me warm.

With him, I blossomed. At last I had found someone who acknowledged my existence. I then became "Pôline". When he spoke my name this way, I felt the magic he breathed into my being.

Yousaf was contemplative by nature. In addition to observing the world with his deep gaze, he analyzed situations before giving an answer. This thinker and dreamer had everything to fascinate me.

With him, I learned not to say anymore from the tips of my lips "I'm fine", but to really feel it from within. At last, I stopped doubting myself at the slightest criticism and developed enough confidence to remain strong when faced with challenges. I also succeeded in calming storms caused by a sense of lacking; I found ways to reduce and stop my suffering.

Together, we discovered the secrets of happiness and changed our thinking by surprising each other and finding the best in ourselves. Yousaf had not been allowed to choose his career path. According to the customs of his country, family ties were of utmost importance, and his grandfather refused to let him leave the city to study elsewhere.

Unable to carry on as a drafter, he sought the recipe for success so he could fulfill his ambitions. Now it was my turn to support him. With courage and determination, he went back to school to become an industrial engineer.

At the end of my business studies, to avoid getting in the way of his goals, I decided to leave Toronto and settle in Montreal. I had no idea what the future held for me, but trusted in my intuition. On his second visit, Yousaf asked me to become his life partner. We were engaged for a year. To better fill the void of his absence and in addition to my work, I enrolled in night school to study psychology.

We got married on December 22, 1969, in the Notre-Dame basilica in Old Montreal. That was the day Pauline Lapointe became Pauline Chiragh. A different sound, evocative of a new world. When my husband talked to me, I sometimes pretended not to hear, because I wanted him to say my name again. This, coming from his lips, became a moving melody. By the tone of his voice, Yousaf gave me wings. Two children were born of this union of two worlds: Sonia and Réjean.

Yousaf's life story

Yousaf was born in Burma (called Myanmar since 1989), a Southeast Asian country framed by Tibet in the north, by China and Thailand in the east, by the Andaman Sea and the Gulf of Siam in the south, and by the Indian Ocean in the west.

When Yousaf was four years old, his family moved to India (part of the British Empire from 1750 to 1947), in a territory that is now the country of Pakistan. He finished his schooling and joined the Indian Air Force to specialize in aeronautical engineering.

After his 17th birthday, he went with his family to live in Cyprus, an island in the Mediterranean Sea. Although this country is geographically close to the Middle East, it is culturally and politically bound to Europe.

At 27 years of age (1960), he left Cyprus to immigrate to England, and then to Canada at 33 years (1966).

Once he had crossed the Atlantic, Yousaf set foot on land in Quebec City on *July 12, 1966*. He was buried in Laval on *July 12, 2005*.

A few months after Yousaf's passing, a great joy came into my life: France, Réjean's wife, gave birth to Eve on October 21. My heart bursting with emotion, I experienced the joy of being a grandmother when I held my granddaughter in my arms. However, it was painful to know that Yousaf would never know that bliss. When he put his hand on France's stomach, he had felt the baby's movements and nicknamed her "Poppy". In the language of flowers, this name symbolizes "a timid ardor", which describes Eve quite well.

Yousaf at 33

CHAPTER 5

The echoes of my nights

Dreams overspread our nights, as we all know. Human history has proven it for every period of our evolution. Since the beginning of time, primitive societies have been struck by the strange, wonderful, amazing, frightful or premonitory character of dreams. According to French medieval historian Jacques Le Goff, it was not until the late twelfth century that knowledge about dreams began moving away from divine or satanic concepts. Our era is characterized by a multitude of studies on dreams and the development of biological or philosophical theories on the matter. Psychiatrist Carl Jung (1875–1961) has illustrated the theory of dreams using a universal language of metaphors and symbols. He claimed that by exploring the depths, we move towards a broader dimension, that of the human soul, experienced through psychic manifestations.[2]

"Within each one of us, there is another being we do not know, but who speaks to us in our dreams. This being tells us how differently he sees us from the way we see ourselves."— Carl Jung (from *Civilization in Transition*, 1958).

Why do we dream? Although several theories have been shared on the true function of dreams, none has been formally adopted. So, we must recognize that no one has managed to break through and understand the meaning of dreams.

A happy life must have meaning. Every day, we encounter many factors which characterize and shape who we are.

These mysterious messages from the soul can sometimes be interpreted as a visit from a spiritual guide coming to lead the way. Interpreting my dreams often helped me to understand the present moment and prepare happier tomorrows. I carefully tended for these dreams; I let them germinate, saw them blossom and flourish. It was then I picked the fruit.

I have always believed that the night is like a messenger. I feel that nightly dreams, unlike daydreams, have guided me without constraints or prohibitions. They helped me understand what was buried deep within me and my memories. A special attention to this dimension of the self can open doors. Often, our life conditions make it difficult to stop and meditate. A dream allows us to reflect on our actions and suggests ways to push the arbitrary limits we impose on ourselves.

"A dream not interpreted is like a letter left unread." (Berachot 55b, excerpt from the Talmud)

Now, I will allow you to discover my story through my dreams...

❧ ❧ ❧

When I was young, I often had the same two dreams. My curiosity got the best of me as I became an adult: I wanted to decipher their meaning.

I have a full wardrobe, tidy and extremely convenient. It's impressive, I would say even sumptuous. I find colourful clothes: dresses, lace, crinolines, knitwear, scarves, coats, shoes and accessories for all occasions. Every time, at the end of the dream, I am left with the illusion of opening a door to a new world.

This dream came from a strong desire to wear new clothes to assert myself. As a child, I found little excitement in the change of seasons because I had seen the same old clothes worn countless times by my sisters. In my family, and elsewhere at the time, clothes were passed on from the eldest to the next in line. Although it was the custom, I felt deprived. I did not have the magnanimity of St. Francis of Assisi. This saintly man, born of a wealthy family, transformed his life by marrying "Lady Poverty" and no longer sought to impress, but was dedicated to sow peace.

At 14, I found a solution to my problem. My mother agreed to let me take sewing lessons. My father, with his refined taste, did not object, since he understood me. Together they arranged for me to receive private lessons with the best seamstress in the village.

At last, I could taste the freedom of making my own clothes. Depending on the season and on my mood, I worked with many different fabrics. How exciting it was to feel the natural beauty of a fabric and to select it for its quality, colour, texture, softness and comfort!

It was through sewing that my sense of creativity emerged; that's how I discovered my artistic side. My sewing teacher knew how to share her expertise. Her constructive comments fostered my self-esteem and sense of aesthetics. I learned to manipulate cloth gently and work out the details with care to ensure a beautiful finished product. The seamstress showed me new techniques, such as ways to make a reversible garment. I enjoyed when she told me: "If you want the result to look like clothes made by a fashion designer, it's up to you to pay attention to subtleties that require ease and dexterity."

The satisfaction of renewing my wardrobe also created a positive impact in my life. Focusing on this work became almost a meditation. I had found a passion that made me lose track of time. Even if we should not judge by appearances, the following also holds true: "If he would take any care of himself and his clothes, he wouldn't look so much like a vagabond." (excerpt from *La Rabouilleuse*, Honoré de Balzac).

A good taste in selecting ensembles and coordinating their colours truly makes a difference. I enjoyed tailoring a cut to my figure, harmonizing shades to my complexion or sometimes bringing out the blue or green of my eyes. Highlighting my eyes gave me a renewed freshness and natural grace; my self-confidence was boosted as I expressed my personality.

I even sewed a vest for my father, which he wore with pride. He knew how to show it off so well that I had to make more for my uncles!

❦ ❦ ❦

My second childhood dream was entirely different. I found myself in an embarrassing situation. I wanted to express myself, but I was unable to utter a single word. Upon awakening, I felt a discomfort, a kind of fever that left me choking.

For example, I'm stuck in a car; I end up in a crowd, where I cannot find the people I was with; or I try to scream, but no sound comes out of my throat.

This choking sensation came from my difficulty with the mind-heart connection, as the throat represents the crossing point between intellect and emotions. I needed to learn to rise above this duality; in other words, to find balance between determination and letting go. I also had to let the energy flow play its catalytic role, so I could better enjoy freedom and peace of mind.

Being the middle child, I often felt uneasy, abandoned, not knowing how to behave. I was the annoying and tiring child who wanted to understand everything. A flood of my questions remained unanswered, because few people bothered. I was never satisfied. Concretely, this obsession followed me, even in my dreams.

These dreams paved the way towards a better knowledge of myself. In 1984, at the age of 42, I began to turn towards preventive rather than curative medicine, since the body cannot be dissociated from the mind, and any weakness indicates a lack of harmony.

◆ ◆ ◆

My son Réjean had a recurring dream that puzzled me for the longest time. On several occasions, during a fever caused by a cold, he dreamt of houses made from cards stacked in pyramids. He saw them fall, one on top of the other. Each time, he woke up feeling disturbed.

Réjean was only four years old when we left Ontario to settle in Quebec. Six months elapsed between the purchase of our new house and the move from our old house. In fact, my husband had moved before the rest of the family. Réjean wondered: "Why is Dad no longer with us?" I told him: "We cannot join your father because we used all the money we have to buy the new house." I needed to find the hidden meaning of his dream. How could I make him understand the reason for this separation—that it was impossible to pay for two properties at once?

Anything we cannot understand remains in our memories and resurfaces in one way or another in our lives. It is through our dreams and nightmares, or sometimes in our daily reactions, that this misunderstanding comes to haunt us until consciousness enlightens us.

My son had another dream, which was just as evocative. He woke up one morning and said to me: "Mom, I was so happy in my dream. I brought my Cabbage Patch doll to school, just like my friends do."

To my surprise, even though I didn't think of myself as sexist, I fell into the same trap as my father. On many occasions, he had told me: "It would be different if you were a boy; are you forgetting that you're a girl?" Even though we had three cars at home, only the boys were allowed to drive them. My sisters and I never had that privilege. My father preferred that we take a taxi.

I was shaken by my son's dream. It made me discover I had the same attitude as my father. How was it that I never thought of offering my son a doll, and yet I bought toy cars for Sonia? So, on the next day off school, of course, we went together to buy a Cabbage Patch doll, and then went out to eat. Back home, Réjean told me: "What a beautiful day! I want to remember it forever."

PART TWO

Entering my dreams

In this second edition, I would like to shed a new light on the chapter about dreams by quoting Carl G. Jung:

Those who learn nothing from the unpleasant facts in their lives, force the cosmic consciousness to play it as many times necessary, to learn what the drama of what happened teaches. What you deny or refuse subdues you... what you accept transforms you.

Being aware of the experience, of the present moment, is a true challenge. So many messages seek to reveal themselves in dreams; they escape us easily. These messages from the unconscious are yet there to help us live better. We must observe, be constantly in touch with our perceptions, and slow down our pace of life to find a perfect balance between body and mind, between introspection and experimentation.

When I was young, I met my father's expectations. I was constantly walking on eggshells. Strangely, despite my extroverted personality, I remained in the shadows, lonely and silent. I did not know how to say "no". At that time, I did not have the same luck as my siblings, that of leaving the family clan to choose my path. My father had given me responsibility for the grocery store. As I was hoping for a future different from the one my father planned for me, I attended night courses while working during the day. In hindsight, however, I must say that since I had started working, I made meaningful connections because I was comfortable with the public. I was not just a saleswoman, I became a friend to my clients, sometimes even a confidante. I learned to observe. I found answers to my questions. My job at the grocery store has therefore helped me better understand human beings and allowed me to develop my creativity and my imagination. I assessed the products, showcased them, and managed the perishable goods. This job also allowed me to gain confidence and independence, to discover my real aspirations. Some people are born with the recipe for happiness; as for me, I took some time to create my own.

I had to quench my thirst for knowledge by reading. This source of joy helped me better perceive the world and its reality. I immersed myself in the author's universe to learn through differences, to help myself adapt to change. I gradually understood that body, soul and spirit were one.

At night, my consciousness was set free. Without any particular knowledge of the universe of dreams, I sought the light and developed my own way of interpreting them. I became, in a way, my own therapist. Through careful inner examination, I found the cause of my discomfort. Thus, interpreting my dreams had become necessary to understand my life experiences.

Dreams are an important part of this book because they have a major influence in my life. These premonitions have encouraged me and still encourage me to remain aware to the rich messages of the unconscious. After long reflections, meaning emerges. Patience and acceptance of a hidden meaning, whether bright and clear or difficult to take in, are the essential prerequisites to properly interpret the subliminal clues. This third eye allows me to take a new look at my life. I continue to observe, to interpret my dreams, to refine my perceptions of what has been done and what remains to be explored.

In the following pages, I therefore open a door on my dreams. I invite you to follow me along a legacy of the heart...

My dreams at a glance

On a sunny day, a songbird perched on the balcony railing and delighted me with a melodious tune.

Re-reading accounts of my nightly dreams awakens touching memories in me, as if I were reading a diary. The first one goes back to 1987. The sequence of my dreams, often a prelude to revelations, coincides with events; this is a sign I was going through periods of intense reflection. Each dream has a near-magical significance. It was thrilling to rediscover these allies of my nights. Each fragment, tinged with meaning, awakens my memory. The adventure back into my past opens doors to my inner wisdom; I have found a new way to enliven my everyday life!

◆

An encounter with Joseph Murphy
Dream of July 24, 1987

I wrote to Joseph Murphy and invited him to my house. He accepts the invitation, so I go meet him at the airport. Sitting by this remarkable man, I am struck by his gaze, a window into the depth of his soul. He says: "I have three days to spend with you. I will give lectures at the location of your choice." I chose Lac-Saint-Jean. I wanted to give people in the region the opportunity to welcome this man, whose great simplicity would remain etched in their memory.

Joseph Murphy (1898–1981) wrote about thirty books. This doctor of philosophy, theology and law was described as a strong proponent of human potential. "It is your Divine right to dramatize, reveal, portray, and express the power, elegance, and riches of the Infinite One."[3] (Excerpt from *Your Infinite Power to be Rich*.)

After this dream, I experimented with Murphy's instructions and benefited from several of them. However, I had to accomplish an inner process. I needed to learn to feel the breath in my body, which would give me the ability to:
- Perceive the first stage in the emotion-triggering process.
- Understand the mechanics of breathing.
- Become aware of the causes behind respiratory blockages.

My other readings led me to discover the theory of Dr. Alexander Lowen (1910–2008). I learnt about bioenergetic analysis, a technique based on the awareness of body movements associated with breathing. It involved detecting blockages and performing anchoring exercises to enable resonance with vital force.

I remember how Dr. Lowen described various methods to facilitate our connection with reality. His theories helped me connect to the present moment in my body, in the areas where sensations emerge. One of the exercises was to go around a table while paying attention to the soles of the feet. "You feel your body and for you to feel your body, your body has to move."[4] (Excerpt from "Interview with Dr. Alexander Lowen" in *The USA Body Psychotherapy Journal*, Volume 7, Number 1, 2008.)

And here I was, looking for an approach to become rooted through breathing. I had to surrender to my inner child, as if I was going outside for a breath of fresh air, striving to breathe better and move towards a gradual revival. I was searching for a simple, yet effective technique. So, for a year, I enrolled in intensive Rebirth sessions.

Here is what the Rebirth approach involves:
• Breathing in a way that is both dynamic and relaxing.
• Feeling the breath through the air exchange, between oxygen and carbon dioxide.
• Creating a close relationship between body and mind.
• Contributing to improved mental clarity.
• Breaking free from physical and psychological blockages.

Conscious breathing maintains a steady and continuous flow of energy. To restore contact between the two cerebral hemispheres, there is no pause between the breath in and breath out. The transition is gradual, resembling an empty moment when the air does not enter or exit. The exercise involves breathing through the nose for an hour without interruption, thereby allowing complete relaxation and letting the body express its memories. Breathing is focused in the upper chest. The person practicing is guided by the air, while remaining aware of passing emotions. The goal is to release the burdens of the past to face fears and attain a better quality of life. Rebirth is a process of personal growth; it must be done with an expert.

It is a matter of using positive affirmations to eliminate self-defeating thoughts. No matter our age, our education or our lifestyle, we are all constantly drawn in by new approaches. We do not always know how to stay connected to our truth. Thus, we do not learn how to improve our breathing; on the contrary, we distance ourselves from the base of vital energy. This theory strongly influenced me.

The Rebirth technique was developed in the 1970s by Leonard Orr, born in 1937. This former student of philosophy and theology was searching for meaning and tended towards a universal approach: to get rid of the death instinct through a close connection with the immortality of the soul. According to him, it is crucial "to be more interested in living than dying and to believe in our trinity."[5]

In 1968, I took correspondence courses in psychology and applied chemistry with the Université du Québec à Montréal. Later, I registered for a course at McGill University called *The World of Chemistry*.

This last course, which I had taken in a foreign language, still did not meet my expectations. I had to put so much energy into it that my son challenged me: "Mom, with all this effort, you're sure to succeed!" Despite all my good intentions and even if I studied using French and English medical dictionaries, I passed with a mere D according to the university's standards. The multiple-choice exam focused on the urgency of intervention, and I was interested in prevention.

As I felt more comfortable with practice than with theory, I moved towards alternative medicine and signed up for a three-year training program in naturopathy.

During this time, I worked part-time as a chiropractor's assistant. This job allowed me to explore another aspect of the human body. But I wanted more; I wanted to find a method that would teach me to develop balance, not only to learn to manage my emotions, but also to process them. I still felt limited in my knowledge.

A new perspective
Dream of December 8, 1987

I meet a young girl on the bus who tells me, "I went to Miami for training to become a medical assistant."

With this dream, I felt I would soon be presented with another opportunity—a new challenge. Still with the goal to understand myself better, I thought of taking an indirect approach: paid work that would widen my perspective, with a combination of allopathic medicine and alternative medicine.

A little while later, my friend Yasmine ran into an old acquaintance, who offered her a work-sharing opportunity as a neurologist's assistant. Because she felt already fulfilled as a housewife, she mentioned to her friend that I would surely be interested. I did not have anything to do. I received a phone call and was offered the job. I truly did not expect to be offered such an opportunity on a silver platter.

My new boss arranged to meet with me. The interview was conducted in English, and we developed a good chemistry from the start. He offered me the job and indicated that I would need to use a dictation machine. I replied: "No problem." But I knew I could not type as fast as he spoke. Although shorthand was part of the program for secretaries, I had to give it up halfway through the course because of my dyslexia. When the letters get mixed up, it's impossible to make out the chaos of words and transcribe them.

My dreams gave me the courage to go beyond my limits and overcome all my fears and apprehensions.

Shorthand
Dream of March 30, 1988

I see myself sitting in a dining room, deep in conversation with my employer. A centrepiece of fruit decorates the table. I softly tell him: "I do not think I can work with the dictation machine." He remains silent, and I feel a gentle kindness in his eyes.

In this dream, the solution became obvious. My colleague could work with the dictation machine in my place. But how could I make such a situation possible? I observed the methods used at my workplace and remembered a conversation where my friend said she liked typing medical reports. Human contact was easy and pleasant for me, so I took the responsibility of answering telephone calls from patients and hospital staff. Thus, the problem was solved, thanks to a fair exchange of duties.

Working in the medical field helped me develop close ties with patients. This sense of closeness promoted comfort in the face of challenges. Sometimes, it helped patients find solutions to their problems. I was determined to reduce their stress and increase my effectiveness. During emergency calls, I could feel their worries about a catastrophic outcome or their fear of a relapse. My role was then to reassure them. I liked to perform duties which gave me the opportunity to put into practice what I was studying in naturopathy.

Often, my doctor was surprised by the information he received from the patients; their confessions indirectly made his work simpler. He said: "I know of no other nurse like you; you seem to have an innate ability for the job." But even though we discussed many different subjects, my studies remained a well-kept secret.

Together, we made a good team. The days went by without breaks. I did my best at work and I was paid accordingly. Since I didn't take any break to eat, very often the patients surprised me with prepared meals or gifts when they returned from their holidays.

What more could I ask for? I worked three days a week and was paid to learn. I travelled by commuter train between my home and my workplace, which gave me time to study. In my last year of training, I started to do part-time consulting, and eventually became an independent professional. This was my last and most rewarding occupation of all.

In the summer of 1992, I knew I was able to demonstrate perseverance, self-reliance and determination. I was convinced that I made the right decision: to assert myself and no longer work for an employer. I wanted to be independent, to follow the impulses of my heart. I strived to experience the thrill of taking the initiative, learn the true meaning of sharing, integrate my philosophy and dream of an openness to the world.

◆

Crying and choking, over a year later
Dream of May 26, 1989

I am a young child, finding myself with my family in a cottage that is not ours. That day, my brothers and sisters are having fun teasing me, and I feel a certain mischief on their part.

I do not like this discomfort; it makes me feel caught in a noose. Wherever I look, I feel them against me. I get so upset that I only have one idea in mind: to disappear. I think about leaving, but I realize they have hidden my handbag and my toothbrush. Furthermore, if I find myself in an unfamiliar place, I could easily get lost. Nevertheless, I still decide to leave. Outside on my own, I begin to cry. As I have no handkerchief, I use tissue paper. I sit on the ground and feel unable to clear my long hair from my face. I moan so strongly that I swallow tissue paper and choke.

At that time, I was taking an evening course named *Getting to know yourself*. I found that work on the self awakens a great many thoughts and analyses.

This dream brings me back to certain stages of my past, at times when I was powerless, feeling unable to react. I needed to take a step back and find the balance between masculine and feminine, while accepting each principle: to find my axis between these two energies. I felt I was finally understanding the anxiety that had filled me since my childhood. My newfound awareness gave meaning to this period of my life—I had to accomplish myself on a whole new level. Leaving the comfort zone brings doubts, fears and uncertainty. Still, I decided to fly on my own and find avenues leading to my path and my truth.

◆

The residence of René Lévesque
Dream of June 6, 1989

A beautiful, vacant house is for sale. It belongs to René Lévesque, and the asking price is $500,000. In front of the entrance, there is a large bookcase with drawers reportedly filled with hidden treasures.

Throughout his life, this politician (23rd premier of Quebec) remained true to his convictions. Such a dream reflected untapped potential for me. I could follow in the footsteps of this great man and pass on the values so dear to my heart to other people. The enthusiasm was there; I only had to wait for the opportunity. And it was on November 22, 1989, that the founder of ORIDIS, an importer of natural products, opened a door to me. He invited me to give my first lecture on the benefits of the Rebirth technique and offer talks on various topics, always pertaining to wellness.

●

Michèle Morgan
Dream of July 16, 1989

I had lent a highchair to a lady that I hardly knew, and later learned that she was the cousin of actress Michèle Morgan. The lady said: "If you want to meet her, I'll give you her contact information." I went to her neighbourhood and when I approached her villa, Ms. Morgan saw me and smiled. Even though I felt like an intruder, I told her about her cousin. I also mentioned how I liked her openness, authentic personality, elegance and simplicity. To my great surprise, Ms. Morgan invited me into her garden for a glass of wine.

After the birth of my daughter Sonia, me and my husband carefully chose an adjustable highchair so we could all get together around the table. At that time, I was beginning to give more and more lectures. This dream prompted me to continue doing so, to speak in small groups around a table, to strengthen exchanges of ideas, to share a common interest with the participants and to delight at their approving glances, as if I were enjoying a good wine.

I had just finished reading the memoirs of Michèle Morgan, written in 1977. She explains how, when she was only three, a friend of her father and amateur astrologer had predicted that she would become famous. Since my childhood, I had always had a special interest for these people whose lives contrasted with mine. The appearance of certain famous individuals in my dreams gave me the chance to expand my perceptions.

❧

The handbag theft
Dream of October 22, 1989

Someone is trying to steal my handbag, specifically my wallet. I scream; the thief panics and runs away as fast as he can.

This dream is loaded with meaning. I express what I feel and assert myself. I defend myself without having to offer any justification, unlike in my childhood dream where no sound came out of my mouth.

❧

Hiding underwater
Dream of February 4, 1990

I find myself in an uncomfortable situation and, to avoid it, I hide under water.

As a child, even though my family had a cottage on the shores of Lac Saint-Jean, I always felt uncomfortable in cold water. When I bathed in the lake, I would lose my breath. So, I interpret this dream as a lesson. Water, the home of the fetus, symbolizes a return to the source. It evokes vitality and regeneration by immersion into the depths of the soul.

●

A high-pitched scream
Dream of June 12, 1990

I am home, and a neighbour rings the doorbell. I open the door. He notices I am alone and leads me to a corner of the room. I do not panic; I find the courage to express myself and let out a high-pitched scream.

The entire household wakes up, and even though I have disturbed their sleep, I am very happy. I feel true liberation. I have no tightness in my throat anymore. Finally, I am able to assert myself as a woman without fearing judgment from others.

This dream was related to the one about the stolen handbag.

● ● ●

It was also by interpreting an initial dream that I found a way to make a wish come true, a wish Yousaf and I held dear to our hearts.

After nine years of marriage, in 1978, I took my first long trip to meet my in-laws. These special moments are forever etched in my heart, as well as in my daughter's. As my son Réjean was only two years old, he stayed in Montreal, where my mother and one of my sisters looked after him. Sonia, aged eight, was old enough to come along with us.

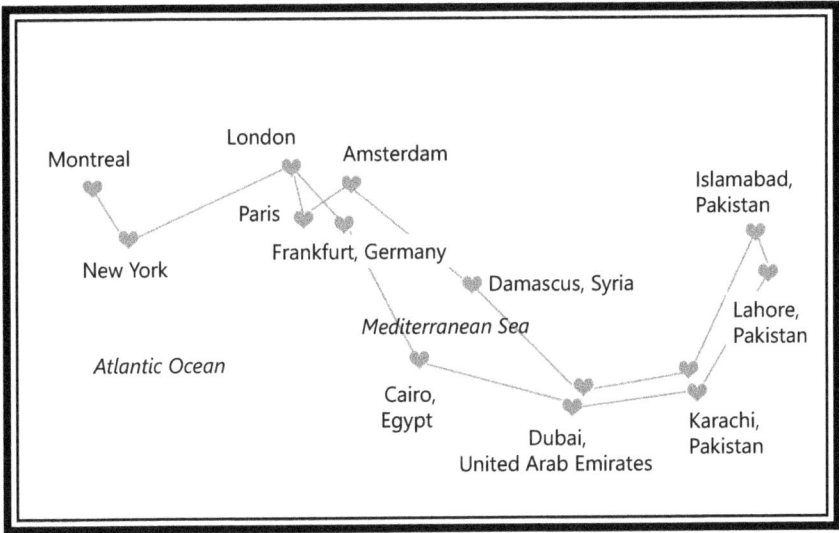

The outbound flight lasted almost 24 hours. This was our route: Montreal to London, London to Paris, Paris to Amsterdam, Amsterdam to Damascus, Damascus to Dubai, Dubai to Karachi, Karachi to Lahore, and Lahore to Islamabad. Because of the delays, it was impossible to know when we would arrive. To welcome us, members of Yousaf's family commuted between their home and the Islamabad airport. In the following years, my husband returned twice to visit his family,

Yousaf often expressed the desire to see the whole family reunited during another trip to the East. As a father, it was important for him to immerse his children in the culture. In 1991, Sonia was a university student, and Réjean was attending a private college. Planning a trip for four people and travelling to the other side of the world seemed almost impossible. Yet...

Here is a series of dreams that acted as trigger events to make the project feasible.

An unexpected dream
Dream of February 4, 1991

One night, the whole family is in the sky, flying like birds. Back on earth, I am impressed by what radiates from our faces.

I felt inside of me that the trip was feasible. We just needed a strategy. Meanwhile, I kept thinking.

◆

Designer clothes
Dream of March 1, 1991

Some people guide my family into a private garden. They leave us near a tree; from there, we see a miniature bridge standing next to a sale of European designer clothes.

Once again, I saw my childhood dream, where I had a full wardrobe. I intuitively felt that these clothes could be easy to acquire. To me, this private garden was a sign of abundance. But it was much more than a memory; this dream was auspicious.

◆

A rainbow
Dream of May 26, 1991

I see a water stream sprout up; a rainbow appears.

This water emerging from deep sources generates impressive force. What's more, the energy of colours creates a bridge between heaven and earth. It also symbolizes a union of the West and the East, bringing about happy events.

●

An enchanting world
Dream of June 6, 1991

What I see is magical: the colours are beyond imagination and cannot be described.

That morning, I was moved by a vision from a subtle world, that of the soul. My two last dreams spoke of initiations. The universe advised me to pay attention to the messages life was sending me to expedite our journey to the East.

In July 1991, my good friend Yasmine had some free time to socialize. She told me that one of her neighbours recently closed her designer boutique for ladies and had a surplus of clothing. The Quebec government had just implemented the provincial sales tax; this increase in retail prices made it difficult for the small business to continue its trade.

As I walked into her place, I was surprised to see she had all a woman could dream of to reinvent her style. The lady suggested to sell her goods at a third of their value and share the profits with me. In addition, each time I managed to sell ten articles of clothing, I was to receive one free. I did not have to think long before agreeing to this profitable offer. With the help of her husband, she brought me a few mobile racks filled with clothes, all bearing the signature of some great designer.

Whenever a customer entered my home, she did not see a living room or dining room, but a ladies' boutique with stunning clothes on display.

At the same time, my acquaintance Emma, who regularly attended Rebirth sessions, was selling lingerie in seniors' residences. She found it difficult to explain to clients how we had to start charging provincial tax in addition to the federal tax, which meant a 15% increase in price, all of a sudden. She brought up the possibility of disposing of her goods, and we agreed. Thus, suitcases full of ladies' undergarments were added to my living room.

The shop quickly gained in popularity. I received calls from women I knew, as well as from women I had never met; all wanted to take advantage of my great deals.

Since I had become a temporary shopkeeper, my husband and I had to redesign the ground floor of our house to make room for the business. Fortunately, this invasion did not disturb the family atmosphere, for the plans we carried in our hearts strengthened our bond.

Yet another idea emerged: that of offering jewellery manufactured in Canada. Although women from the East wear gold jewelry, they also enjoy completing their outfits with costume jewelry. So, I asked my clients and friends to give me their worn-out jewelry. It was Yousaf's turn now to open a workshop. With patience, he took pleasure in giving back character to the tarnished jewels. He used recipes passed down from his mother to add sparkle to the brooches, necklaces, pins and medallions. He took great pride in opening his box full of glittering ornaments and let the young ladies choose among them.

During a phone call with my sister-in-law, I asked her what she would like as a gift from Canada. To my surprise, she asked for bras, explaining that the women in her country were fascinated by the beauty of our undergarments. At that time, the majority of them made their own underwear. So, I started negotiating what was left of the lingerie.

Meanwhile, I had gained experience in naturopathy, and an entire floor was reserved for my consultations. My business was registered under the name of Pauline Lapointe-Chiragh, N.D. enr., and later evolved into a naturopathic school. Through my recent encounters, I was also able to market my business and acquire new clients or future students.

To travel to Pakistan, we still had to purchase tickets, so we took a new mortgage on the house. Sonia and I left Quebec in November 1991 to embark on this great adventure. Yousaf and Réjean joined us later, during the holiday season.

Before our departure, I received Mona, another client from Rebirth sessions. She was a sales representative for a candy company. When I told her about our travel plans, she said: "Your husband should not arrive empty handed; let me take care of that." A few days later, Mona returned with several boxes. Believe it or not, Yousaf's suitcase for the trip contained practically just sweets. Wherever he went, he did not offer flowers, but chocolates.

Those premonitory dreams, packed with information, were like pieces of a puzzle. I only had to assemble them, while being on the lookout for signs of destiny, which appeared almost as if by magic.

Réjean, aged 15, was on his first trip to Pakistan. As for Sonia, she returned this time with an adult's perspective. Compared to what they had experienced in Quebec, my children were astonished to suddenly discover that their father had been raised and educated in an opulent environment. The grandfather was very different from his son: fiery by nature, he always enjoyed impressing us.

We were transformed, resplendent; our eyes radiated happiness. A professional stylist could not have done better to enhance our features. We all wore refined clothes and brought back gifts galore. The Chiraghs from Canada were very proud of the fruits of their efforts and of their achievements. But for my father-in-law, this was only natural. He had been the head tailor for the officers of the army which, until 1947, had belonged to the British Empire. Under a fixed employment contract, he moved from one military base to another. His lifestyle, influenced by his social standing, reflected prosperity.

Not only did we look like a princely family, but we were also treated with great dignity. To my father-in-law, a very endearing man, no ambition was too wild. He could read into our eyes and was capable of inspiring dreams.

For some outings, he wanted us to dress according to the customs of the country. He was always happy to contact the tailor. He even took us to the dyer so that he could coordinate the colours of the clothes with our complexion. And of course, the clothes fit us perfectly.

When we woke up in the morning and made even the slightest noise, a servant rang the doorbell to offer us tea. We would not enter our bedroom with our shoes on; we left them at the door. The next day, we would find them polished like new.

We mostly travelled with a private chauffeur. Yet for large family outings, we needed several more to accommodate everybody.

We were astonished to discover the beauties of the land. The impressive Taj Mahal epitomizes Muslim art in India. Its construction began in 1631 under Emperor Shah Jahan, in memory of his wife who died at 39 years as she birthed her fourteenth child. This crown palace, a symbol of eternal love, sparkles under the Indian sun, changing colours depending on the time of day. It has been registered as a UNESCO world heritage site since 1983. The archaeological site of Mohenjo-Daro is a mystery even today. The Indus Valley, the cradle of Indian civilization located northeast of Karachi, is a vestige of one of the greatest cities from India's Bronze Age. Another town named Thatta, near Karachi, is well known for its historical monuments. This capital of three successive dynasties reflects the civilization of Sindh, a province of Pakistan. It is the home of breathtaking mountains. The city of Lahore is still the cultural capital, whereas Islamabad, near Rawalpindi, has become the country's political and economic centre. This city was built between 1960 and 1963 by Europeans.

Our emotions were difficult to put into words because we also travelled within ourselves, coming into contact with the history of humankind. We enjoyed every moment and were happy to be there, sharing a daily life so different from our own. For instance, the air was often filled with an aroma of spices that created a pleasant scent. Strolling through the streets, we were charmed by the fragrance of Indian jasmine flowers. This was the same perfume that conquered Cleopatra when she went to meet Marcus Antonius (one of Julius Caesar's officers) on a boat whose sails were covered with jasmine oil. And the streets—what a sight. In addition to automobiles, public roads were crowded with pedestrians, carts pulled by donkeys, bicycles, scooters, motorcycles and multicoloured buses.

We could easily sleep under the stars on the roof of the house. We used beds made from twine wrapped around wooden frames; these beds also served as tables or benches. Since they fit well one inside another, they were easily stored in a closet. Inviting guests overnight never seemed to be a problem.

These family reunions will forever stay in our memories. Despite our differences, our many similarities brought us closer; everywhere we went, we felt at home.

The adventure even strengthened the bonds between us. As Sonia and I had started and ended our trip earlier than Yousaf and Réjean did, we returned with different memories. In addition to his school holidays, Réjean took two more weeks of vacation; he and his father returned at the end of January. Our dream had come true. When we talked about it later, we felt that we enjoyed the adventure for all it had to offer. The dream of the rainbow had prepared me to experience this visit, filled with colours in every aspect, at full intensity.

Upon returning from my trip, I continued to improve myself by learning about varied energy techniques such as therapeutic touch, Reiki and radiesthesia. It was at this time that I learned that I had a fibroma in the uterus, a benign tumour formed by fibrous tissue.

—◆—

Radiant warmth
Dream of August 17, 1992

I notice a rash on my face; I manage to make it disappear. While performing a Rebirth, I cough and I approach the sink; secretions emerge from my throat. At the same time, I feel warmth at the spot where the fibroma is located. This warmth is intense, not at skin level, but in the layers of the epidermis. I feel it like a gentle flame, radiating heat deep within me.

I realized that if I was responsible for this intruder in my body, it was up to me not to let myself be overcome and to eliminate it.

At night, I fell asleep while focusing my thoughts on my uterus. Without pressure, I put my hands on my belly, imagining a fluid emerging from this lump. Since I knew that the brain is less active at night and that the subconscious is constantly working, I decided to put my mind to my service. Every evening, I repeated the same scenario until I felt warmth with the same intensity as in my dream. Time passed on, and I became able to quickly locate the radiation under my hands.

One evening, finding myself in a doze, I felt a source of light emanating from my solar plexus. It refreshed my whole being. When I returned to the doctor, the fibroma had disappeared.

The three doors
Dream of December 22, 1992

I see several doors ajar in a room. Afterwards, three of them open before me.

This dream confirmed the concepts I had learned while studying the philosophy of naturopathy—the body cannot be separated from either the spirit or the soul.

In addition to offering private consultations, Rebirth sessions and massage therapy, I started teaching. From this dream, I gained a better understanding of human potential. I also recognized the strength of learning through the action of sharing.

There are three initiatory doors leading to different passages, three possibilities to discover what lies beyond. I should no longer remain trapped, unable to decide between two doors, imprisoned by the fear of change. I needed to go forth and no longer feel locked out or barricaded. First, I had to cross the threshold and go within to access wisdom. From the first door, I could see the rising sun, the centre, the here and now. From the second door, I saw light and shadow, an opportunity for choice. Finally, the last door, that of the setting sun, allowed me to step back, stop and think.

I had to learn to use my spirit as an intermediary to reach my heart, to follow my inspirations and tap into my potential. Then, I had to let rise what lay deep within me and put my professional training into practice. I had to satisfy my curiosity and discover what has haunted me since my childhood. Furthermore, I needed to share my discoveries. Seeing my customers regain their light gave me strength to achieve other goals.

I received a multitude of messages through coincidences and random events in my daily life. I had found my way, I just had to let myself be guided to explore new avenues. Although the road seemed long, I saw a light appear on the horizon. "Spiritual health is manifested in dreams having a divine origin," said historian Jacques Le Goff.

The stacked cones
Dream of February 7, 1993

I see a series of boxes and cones stacked in perfect order.

My ideas became clearer and took shape. When the mind and intelligence of the heart are channeled through the body, everything fits together and is aligned in perfect unity.

◆

Awareness of an earthquake
Dream of April 9, 1993

I am inside the house; the earth shakes. During this short period, my body resonates with another vibration; I quiver in every fiber of my being. When I become aware of this, I look at the people around me and realize that I am the only one to have felt this event.

I realized that the desire for self-fulfillment was not a shameful disease. Instead, I was just lucky to have found my way. When people teasingly called me "crunchy", I had to be careful not to let my little self take over. Of course, at the beginning, I sometimes annoyed my family with all my excitement. I occasionally was blunt with certain truths and received unpleasant reactions. While continuing my work, I continued to learn and gravitated towards homeopathy.

I was particularly fascinated when I discovered the flower remedies of Dr. Edward Bach (1886–1936). Dr. Bach was homeopath with a sensitive, idealistic and mystical view. He devoted his life to searching for true medicine free of harmful processes, a medicine that could heal both mind and body, without separating the two. Dr. Bach firmly believed that every disease had its source in the psychic realm. For him, healing could only be done by removing the root cause of illness, by treating the patient and not the disease.

He began to use wildflowers from fields and forests to relieve suffering, avoiding the use of toxic plants. He identified seven families of emotional states: fear, uncertainty, oversensitivity, insufficient interest in present circumstances, loneliness, resignation and despair. He developed thirty-eight flower essences as well as the "Rescue Remedy", which all contribute to a better physical and emotional balance. "Suffering is the result of a cry of the soul,"[6] he said. (Translated excerpt from *Manuel complet des quintessences florales du Dr Edward Bach: Initiation, perfectionnement*, 2011.)

A giant leap
Dream of October 16, 1993

Someone pushes me into the water. I get up with a giant leap, reaching the other side of the pool. People look at me with astonishment. Then, I pass through a wall and continue floating.

This dream got me into a state of wonder; I allowed myself to be carried away by this wave of wellness. My heart, head and body merged, combining feelings, ideas and images. My spirit, in union with the five senses, entered the flow of consciousness, creating magnetic forces and breaking all boundaries so I could take on a new challenge.

A voluminous book
Dream of November 13, 1993

I hold a voluminous book in my hands. I spend hours flipping through the pages and studying the content. I become very selective in my reading, just as if I were reconstructing each chapter.

I perceived this dream as a way to put some order in my life, a form of spring cleaning within me. I let go of false beliefs and experienced a strong sense of lightness. But the dream was much more than that: it was a second premonitory dream. I had to give myself time. Thoughts emerged, took shape and bore fruit. After thinking it over, I decided to write this book.

◆

Dad's visit
Dream of February 17, 1994

I see my father (deceased in 1977) entering through the window. He is relaxed and has his coat open. Our eyes meet and he makes his way towards me. His expression, I notice, is full of kindness. Words are not necessary; we understand each other in silence.

He came to greet me on his birthday. My father epitomized the man of his time. He would say: "Life is all about work." But that night, I was visited by the ideal father.

◆

Energy
Dream of April 3, 1994

When I give a massage to someone, I witness what appears to be a rejuvenation process. Perhaps the improved oxygenation restores vigour and energy to the entire body.

Remembering the famous words of Albert Einstein—everything is vibration—I have carried for some time an intuitive vision that unites me to the laws of the universe.

During Reiki trainings, I asked students to make drawings interpreting three stages of life: childhood, the present, and their vision of the future. Without words and through trivial gestures, each student revealed significant milestones in their life story, as well as signs of their will to transform this story and live better.

When I did this exercise myself, I pictured myself in the future with open arms, carrying a candle in my hand. I was surprised to see my drawing, full of meaning, revealing light and energy. In the blink of an eye and without any brainstorming, on November 17, 1994, I named my business Luminergie (combination of French words for *light* and *energy*). As time went on, I offered new courses at my Centre. I had many dreams in which I was giving birth to a baby. In fact, the writing process for each textbook was a form of childbirth.

❦

Lymph drainage
Dream of July 23, 1994

I am abroad taking a course on lymph drainage.

I say to myself: "Stay alert to anything that might appear as a gift from life." It was another premonitory dream.

◆

Encounter with Chantal Poulin
Dream of August 2, 1994

I am giving a massage to artist Chantal Poulin's father. He says: "I'll give you a painting, because I also paint." I did not want to displease him, but I didn't want a painting by him. I wanted one by Chantal. Then I saw her husband, and ultimately the radiant painter herself, dressed in white.

I interpreted this dream as a possibility to contact Chantal Poulin. Days went by, and one day I was surprised to see her at an exhibition, dressed in white. Stunned, I wondered how to approach her. Albert Einstein said: "Coincidence is God's way of remaining anonymous." I went up to her, and we smiled at each other. Then, not knowing what to say, I quickly told her about my dream. She said: "You come at the right time, I was about to take a break. Do you want to come with me?" Energy flowed between us. Later, she came to experience a few Rebirth sessions at my school and told me some of her dreams. We developed a friendship, and I even had the pleasure of visiting her studio to see her at work. She commented: "Pauline has a very personal way to understand others. She has the ability to see us from the inside, as no one else can. After a brief meeting where she analyzed one of my dreams, she could perceive the most intimate part of me. She knows how to understand the mirror of the soul. Pauline really has a great talent!"

Baptism
Dream of August 21, 1994

I enter a place to attend a baptism, but it is not in a church. The priest and the guests are dressed in white cloaks. During the ceremony, I see a halo around the baby's head.

This dream was the harbinger of renewal, of a transition towards purification of the soul. The psychologist and French writer Jacques Salomé, born in 1935, has written many books on communication. He stated: "We spend our lives being born into the world."

The power of light
Dream of September 4, 1994

I feel gravity pulling down my limbs, my body is heavy. Then, in a flash, a light is born and everything emerges; I become light as a feather. The air I breathe fills my heart with happiness.

I enjoyed a sense of liberation. The weight I carried within me was almost gone, and a new feeling took over my body. I felt rejuvenated.

These experiences led me towards more intuitive states of consciousness, as well as an evolution towards spiritual development with a universal aspect.

◆

Confidence at the wheel
Dream of November 6, 1994

I drive for a long time in the fast lane of the highway and pass several cars.

I felt freedom and power, like a galloping horse. I was in full control of the vehicle, without any constraints. I felt wonderfully transported by the fluidity of movement.

◆

Mother Teresa
Dream of January 20, 1995

I am on holiday. Someone comes to me and says that Mother Teresa lives nearby. To visit her, I have to follow a very narrow road leading to a small house. When I find myself in front of her, I see her surrounded by children. Our eyes meet. I feel a combination of joy and tenderness. She walks over to me and blesses me.

I felt this dream as an inspiration. Mother Teresa is an example of dedication, always ready to help. She offers her heart to love and her hands to serve.

◆

An unexpected visit
Dream of March 13, 1995

Someone rings the doorbell. And how surprised I was to see my in-laws from the East! Uninformed of their arrival, I feel euphoric. I still cannot believe they are before me.

I understood this premonitory dream a while later. I had to dare to go beyond the known boundaries.

◆

Mountain-peak enthusiasts
Dream of July 25, 1995

I am in the United States, sitting with a lady in a restaurant. She is describing magnificent places known only to alpine skiers and adds that, for those who love the high summits, skiing is a lifestyle. She states that the waiting lists to visit these special places span over five years. She concludes by saying: "When you want to live a dream, the concept of time is irrelevant."

This second dream, carrying the same symbol of the unexpected, transported me to the East and to the United States. I took it as a sign of renewal.

It was summer, and the vacation time inspired me to let go. I took the opportunity to spend a week at a spa. I let myself be pampered and, in my spare time, I attended conference workshops. One of them was about breathing, so I added my two cents and spoke of Rebirth.

Later, a woman with a pretty smile and a foreign accent came up to me. The discussion became alive, as we shared common interests. The course of the conversation changed, and she asked me if it was possible to continue talking in my room. I assumed she wanted to experience Rebirth. I had no intention of becoming a therapist for a night because I wanted to enjoy this time to rest. I thought of the best way to refuse without offending her, but I was in for a surprise. I learned that she lived in Switzerland; the purpose of her trip was to combine business and leisure by discovering some disciplines practised in Quebec. As head of continuing education for adults, she was looking for teachers for the small university of Lausanne in the Vaud canton. After reading the brochure for my Luminergie centre and spending time with me, she offered me to come and teach Reiki and ear hygiene, as well as to give private Rebirth consultations.

On September 11, 1995, I started teaching at the *Université populaire de Lausanne*, an institution striving to transmit theoretical and practical knowledge to everyone. I taught there for four weeks. In my leisure time, I took advantage of invitations to explore the area and discover German-and Italian-speaking Switzerland. I was fascinated by the beauty of the mountains and their peaks. I was lucky to teach in a foreign country, and the experience was memorable.

❧

A change of vision
Dream of October 12, 1995

I am in a funeral home. Every time I approach the coffin, I see the deceased person blink, and a purple glow appears over her body. To understand this phenomenon, I repeat my action a few times—the same vision appears. I go back one last time. The deceased person opens her eyes and comes out of the coffin, very slowly and naturally.

I felt that this dream was a good omen. It inspired me to take on a new perspective and develop another way of thinking or working. Or simply, it led me to stop, look and listen, using the power of my imagination.

◆

Flowers on the steps
Dream of December 10, 1995

I am preparing for my wedding. My garments include a white cape with a royal-blue hood trimmed with white fur. I ask my fiancé Yousaf to lay flowers on the steps we would be climbing.

This dream was also prophetic. The annual convention held by the *Ordre des naturothérapeutes du Québec* (Quebec naturopathic association) was planned for the following week. As an honorary member, I received a medal of recognition at the tribute ceremony.

◆

The boat captain
Dream of January 2, 1996

I complete my training to learn to operate a boat. I am happy to receive the results, which indicate I am ready to become a captain.

This dream was another harbinger of change that I was also experiencing on a daily basis. It was as if the Luminergie centre had expanded more than I had hoped for.

At that time, our team included twelve people, both teachers or coordinators in different regions: Saguenay-Lac-Saint-Jean, Quebec City, Gaspésie and Mont-Laurier. I also had two volunteer contributors.

I promoted my school using word-of-mouth and leaflets. To increase the visibility of my company, I rented booths at exhibitions and conferences dedicated to health and wellness. The centre's success depended on the cooperation and involvement of all my family members. Each played a role by participating in the school's outstanding prosperity.

In order to thrive, businesses must depend on a multidisciplinary group. Their fulfillment comes from internal and external factors which foster personal development for all. Each student motivated me to deepen my knowledge on health and quality of life.

On May 31, 1996, the Luminergie centre in Laval was officially recognized as a naturopathic school by the government of Quebec; the federal government followed suit on September 4. On June 30 of the same year, I was officially accepted in the doctoral program in naturopathy I had applied to. I chose to write my thesis on the journey of the spirit.

◆

Inability to understand
Dream of May 7, 1997

I wake up and see a close-up of the number 8, but I do not understand what it means. That number 8 flashes multiple times as it becomes smaller and smaller.

This number symbolizes two polarities, yin and yang, the spiral of our DNA, a vessel of creative movement. It was a cryptic message. On the earthly plane, the figure eight horizontally forms a loop, a knot to undo, but which one? This dream, like the one about the boat captain, had me intrigued: did it symbolize a pause? I was unable to grasp its meaning.

◆

Friday, June 13, 1997, the Canadian Grand Prix for the Formula One World Championship race was held in Montreal. The race was certainly memorable for many, but for me, it was the day my fortunes turned around. While crossing at an intersection, I was hit by an automobile. This violent thrust carried me into an altered state: everything seemed to happen in slow motion. Although I was conscious and nothing appeared to escape me, I remained indifferent to what was going on. My body seemed separate from reality. I felt no pain, but when I arrived at the hospital, the rolling of the wheels of the stretcher on the floor tiles brought me back into the present moment—I had severe pain and chills.

My right humerus was broken, so I underwent surgery. Three pins were needed to hold my arm together. I was hospitalized for ten days. It was then that I discovered a world previously unknown to me.

At the time, the Quebec government was making budget cuts in health services. Nurses were offered the option to retire early; many of them seized the opportunity. This situation upset the workers, both physically and emotionally.

Normally, in the field of education, summer is a time of rest, filled with hope. But this event changed my plans. For a while, life took another direction: I had to depend on others to survive. My brain made me feel as if I had fallen back to a primitive state. My schedule was filled with rehabilitation sessions, physiotherapy and motor skills exercises. I made efforts daily to become functional again, and restore suppleness and elasticity to my wounded body.

I had several dreams during this period, but having lost track of time, I did not note the dates.

●

The crystal Eiffel Tower

I see a beautiful crystal statuette of the Eiffel Tower. I turn it in all directions; the sun's rays project rainbows through the quartz stone.

Crystal is a symbol of transparency and transformation; it is also a symbol indicating long personal labour. The Eiffel Tower, by its height, gives an improved perspective. I still wonder how this was relevant to me, as I had difficulty grasping the meaning of this dream.

◆

The star of David

I see the Seal of Solomon, also known as the star of David. Six branches form two triangles, one ascending and the other descending.

My strength returned gradually and I regained more autonomy. I was also aware that I was at a crossroads. The memory of the drawing that inspired the name for my Luminergie centre continued to call upon me: it was a representation of the future, arms open to the sky with a candle in one hand. The image evoked momentum as well as strength and transformation.

The dreams continued, showing similarities and revealing coherent connections.

◆

New harvest

I am in the countryside, admiring the blue sky. Often, I recognize in the meadows the blue-green foliage of spring, but nothing is ready for picking. Then I walk through a freshly plowed

105

field. I walk quietly along the furrows, looking downwards as if I were searching for a grain of wheat.

These dreams indicate a new path to follow, but which one?

My recovery continued. One day, Sonia came to visit and offered me a book with simple texts strongly emphasizing the primordial role of our habitat on our well-being. This book spoke of harmony through Feng Shui: the art of living better in one's space by letting the energy flow like a dance, in order to make the home a haven of peace. I felt an energy of inspiration flow through me.

In the memory of my drawing, I no longer saw a candle in my hand, but a torch glowing with a higher intensity. I felt that a door was opening, a door that had remained closed until now. This door led to the world of business. I was ready for a new challenge; it was time to venture onto new paths. I had just discovered the submerged part of the iceberg.

Acknowledgments

I would like to express my gratitude to the loved ones who have awakened me and guided me along a winding road. Even if we only spent brief moments together, some of you have left a mark which will never fade.

A special thanks to those who, in the past, allowed me to fulfill myself. I am grateful for your trust. So often, it's your encouragement that kept me going.

I send out my gratitude to my dear friends, especially Pierrette Henn and Éliette Simard, always so loyal. I also am grateful towards my mentors and friends, Michel De Vos and Didier Combatalade. For several years, you have worked in the shadows, so kindly offering me your support.

I keep a lasting memory of the wonderful trio uniting me and my two faithful coordinators, Claire Duhot from Quebec City and Francine Bourbeau from Montreal.

I could never be thankful enough for Marie Dupuis. You are the one who brightened my Wednesdays in recent years with spontaneous writing workshops and encouraged me to dare this adventure!

To Alice Champagne, your generous support throughout this project also helped me progress.

A warm thank you goes out to Hira Masood and Evelyn L. Schofield, B.A., for your contribution to the English version of this book.

Finally, I would like to thank the late Father Benoît Lacroix, an extraordinary man who touched my life. With his attentive listening and insight, he made valuable suggestions and allowed me to complete this work serenely.

Biography of Pauline Lapointe-Chiragh

1942   On August 19, Pauline Lapointe was born in Saint-Cœur-de-Marie, a small village in the administrative region of Saguenay-Lac-Saint-Jean in Québec. She is the fifth daughter of Jos-Nil Lapointe and Germaine Gilbert.

1951   Moved to Normandin not far from her place of birth.

1961   Elected Queen of the Dolbeau Carnival.

1966   Moved to Toronto.

1966   Met Yousaf, her future husband.

1980   Returned to Québec in Sainte-Dorothée, Laval.

1985   Began her naturopathic studies (which she continued until 1988); worked as a part-time receptionist in a neurologist's office.

1992   Became a full-time naturopathic consultant.

1993   Opened her school of naturopathy, Luminergie.

1995   Travelled to teach in Lausanne, Switzerland.

1996   Luminergie got accredited by the federal and provincial governments.

2001   Became Doctor in Naturotherapy, Academy of Sciences and Research of Montréal.

2005   Yousaf passes away.

2007   Worked as tour leader for three health trips to Romania.

2014   Publishes the French version of *Au seuil d'une porte*. First launch at The Chesterfield Hotel in Palm Beach, Florida; second launch at the Mordecai-Richler Library in Montréal. Participated in the Saguenay-Lac-Saint-Jean Book Fair. At a tribute evening, a gift box of her book was presented in luxury binding.

2014   Gives a lecture on Transmission through Writing. Intergénération Québec.

2014   Took training to start a business, with the Marguerite-Bourgeoys school board.

2015   Led four writing workshops at Relais Famille.

2015   Participated in an interview at Émergence meditation center.

2015   Gave a lecture at the Marc-Favreau library.

2017   Gave a lecture on writing therapy, Centre for Seniors, Villeray.

2017   Coordinated the translation of *Au seuil d'une porte* and published the bilingual book, *On the way in*.

2017   Took training on the sale and distribution of a book.

2017   Lectured on leadership for a business start-up program at the Commission scolaire de Montréal.

Biography of Massoud Golriz
Painter

Born in the land of the Silk Road, Massoud Golriz studied painting at the *École nationale supérieure des Beaux-Arts* in Paris before immigrating to Quebec in the 1980s.

While he was studying architecture at the *Université de Montréal*, the director of the faculty recognized in him a rare talent in free-expression drawing.

His paintings evoke an aquatic or vegetal world, a profusion of forms in the style of Persian miniatures. His art is expressed on silk fabrics and most often displayed in the form of wall hangings, folding screens or curtains.

www.golriz-design.com

Biography of Hira Masood

Citizen of Yousaf's country, Hira Masood studied foreign languages at the University of Modern Languages (NUML) in Islamabad, Pakistan.

She later worked at the *Alliance Française d'Islamabad* as a French teacher and librarian, and concurrently as a French lecturer at NUML.

She had an urge to learn the French language; this deep and inspiring desire became a reality when she experienced French culture while walking in the streets of Paris. Hard work and persistence allowed her to translate this French book without losing its essence.

Hirra.masood@yahoo.com

Epilogue

At the age of 70, I underwent a complete medical examination, since I felt an ever-present urge to reassure myself about my health. Many people around me who were struggling with fragile health endured difficult times. After the examination, my physician told me: "Madam, please come back when you're a hundred years old!" That night I fell asleep crying: "Thirty more years to live! To be happy, I must take a new turn in life."

It is my husband who came to see me in a dream and initially gave me the courage to go ahead with this project. The meaning of his message was clear: "Let your goal become the mission of your life."

After many years of hard work, I published my first book Au seuil d'une porte *in spring 2014.*

Then, a decisive meeting with Father Benoît Lacroix opened me a new path, giving me a new threshold to cross. "Why not publish a bilingual version?" he suggested. His trust in me gave me the impetus to undertake the translation of my book. And it is this momentum that we find in the title that I have chosen, On the way in. *The cover is almost the same; I added the picture of my two grandchildren who are so dear to my heart.*

I learned a lot by coordinating the translation work. Of course, I have encountered many difficulties, but I also faced interesting challenges and had a lot of fun. Although it is the same book, this one may have a totally different life: I want it to travel through time and space...

www.ingramcontent.com/pod-product-compliance
Lightning Source LLC
Chambersburg PA
CBHW060509280326
41933CB00014B/2902